Manual Of The Cambridge School For Girls: Setting Forth The Plan Of The School And The Conditions Under Which Pupils Are Admitted

Cambridge School For Girls

In the interest of creating a more extensive selection of rare historical book reprints, we have chosen to reproduce this title even though it may possibly have occasional imperfections such as missing and blurred pages, missing text, poor pictures, markings, dark backgrounds and other reproduction issues beyond our control. Because this work is culturally important, we have made it available as a part of our commitment to protecting, preserving and promoting the world's literature. Thank you for your understanding.

MANUAL OF THE CAMBRIDGE SCHOOL FOR GIRLS, SETTING FORTH THE PLAN OF THE SCHOOL AND THE CONDITIONS UNDER WHICH PUPILS ARE ADMITTED. CAMBRIDGE, MASSACHUSETTS.
M DCCC XC VIII

Director: MR. ARTHUR GILMAN

MANUAL

OF

THE CAMBRIDGE SCHOOL

Learning teaches more in one year than experience in twenty.—ASCHAM

Knowledge is of no use without intelligence. What is the use of lighting additional candles for the blind?—R. H. QUICK

Study depends upon the will, and the will does not endure restraint.—QUINTILIAN

Founded A. D. M DCCC LXXX VI

Cambridge, Massachusetts

M DCCC XC VIII

Some men, friendly enough of nature, but of small judgment in learning, do think I take too much pains and spend too much time in setting forth these children's affairs; but these good men were never brought up in Socrates' school, who saith plainly that no man goeth about a more godly purpose than he that is mindful of the good bringing up both of his own and other men's children.
    ROGER ASCHAM (1563), in *The Schoolmaster*.

Love is fitter than fear, gentleness better than beating, to bring up a child rightly in learning.
    ROBERT ASCHAM (1563), in *The Schoolmaster*.

How many good and clear wits of children be nowadays punished by ignorant schoolmasters!
    SIR THOMAS ELYOT (1531).

If we must cleave to the eldest, and not the best, we should be eating acorns, and wearing old Adam's pelts.
    RICHARD MULCASTER (1582).

The essential principle of education is not teaching — it is love.
    JOHN HENRY PESTALOZZI (1799).

I do not think that any language, be it whatsoever, is better able to utter all arguments, either with more pith or greater plainness, than our English tongue is.
    RICHARD MULCASTER (1582).

SCHOOL MOTTO. Chosen by the pupils.
"*Truthe and gentil dedes.*" — CHAUCER.

Matters set forth.

The Calendar	4
The Aim of the School	5
The Buildings	6
The Teachers Specialists	6
The Classes Small	6
No petty Rules of Behavior	7
Opportunities for Conference with Parents	7
Overmuch Home Study Deprecated	7
Progress to be Steady, but not Rushing	8
The Importance of the Study of English	8
The old-fashioned art of Reading Aloud	9
The Departments	
The Academic Department	10
The Classical Course	11
The Graduate Course	11
The Preparatory Department	12
The course to be fitted to each pupil	12
Terms for Day Pupils	13
Terms for Resident Pupils	14
The Home Life	15
Cultivation not learned from Books	16
Advantages of studying in Cambridge	16
The Family Circles Small	19
Lectures, Readings, Concerts, etc.	20
The School Work	21
The Academic Department	21
English Courses	21
History	23
Vocal Training	24
Mathematics	25
German	26
French	26
Chemistry	28
Physics	29
Geology	29
Zoölogy	30
Physiology	30
Psychology	30
Botany	30
Astronomy	31
Drawing	31
The Fine Arts	31
The Classical Course	32
Latin	33
Greek	34
The Preparatory Department	
English	36
German	37
French	37
Mathematics	37
Geography	38
Zoölogy	39
Natural History	39
Physiology	39
Botany	39
Special Work	40
The Situation of the School	41

The Calendar.

1898.

September 29. Thursday. CHRISTMAS TERM begins.
    New pupils report at the School House, the previous day at 9 A. M. for classification.

Nov. 24. Thursday. Thanksgiving. (Holiday.)

Dec. 16. Friday. Close of Christmas Term.

The Christmas Recess.

1899.

Jan. 3. Tuesday. EASTER TERM begins.

Feb. 22. Wednesday. Washington's Birthday. (Holiday.)

March 23. Thursday. Easter term closes.

The Easter Recess.

April 5. Wednesday. SPRING TERM begins.

April 19. Wednesday. Patriots' Day. (Holiday.)

May 30. Tuesday. Memorial Day. (Holiday.)

June 8. Thursday. School closes for the long vacation.
    Pupils who are to take College admission examinations are tutored for a few days longer.

The Long Vacation.

Sept. 28. Thursday. CHRISTMAS TERM begins.
    New pupils report the previous day at 9 A. M. for classification.

Nov. 30. Thursday. Thanksgiving.

Dec. 15. Friday. Close of Christmas Term.

1900.

Jan. 2. Tuesday. EASTER TERM begins.
    Pupils are to be present at 8.50 o'clock of every day, not a holiday, and to remain until the end of every school session.

"The framing of the mind craveth exquisite consideration." — RICHARD MUL-CASTER (1582), *Sometime teacher of the poet Spenser.*

THE CAMBRIDGE SCHOOL
NO. 36 CONCORD AVENUE,
CAMBRIDGE, MASS.

THE aim of THE CAMBRIDGE SCHOOL is to give substantial and well-ordered instruction to girls and young women. The intention is to arrange for every pupil a course of study adapted to her peculiar needs, providing for those who do not intend to go to college as carefully as for those who have a collegiate career in prospect. The Director is Mr. Arthur Gilman.

The Teachers Many, Classes Small.

The School occupies three sunny buildings in the residential part of Old Cambridge. Two of these are residences for young ladies who come from a distance. The third is the School Building proper, which contains the class-rooms, study-rooms, dressing-rooms, book-room, laboratories, art-rooms, and office. The building receives the unobstructed light of the sun on all sides, and there are no obscure rooms or passages. The whole of the building is evenly heated by means of hot water, and is thoroughly ventilated. The walls are adorned with casts, and are colored in tints restful to the eye. The seats of the pupils, in class-rooms and study-rooms, are so arranged that the light falls upon their books at the best angle for the eyes.

The teachers are specialists, chosen for ability in their particular departments. The number engaged makes it possible to have the classes small and the work effective. It is intended to use those modern methods which have stood the test of experience.

Home Study to be Reduced.

Applicants for admission are supposed to be willing to study, and not to require petty rules of behavior. Those who are not prepared to work in harmony with their teachers are not desired as pupils and will not be retained. It is intended to teach the pupils how to study, and to cultivate in them the habits of application and the self-control requisite to true womanly character. The pupils are taught that study is work, but that it is agreeable work.

Teachers are in attendance at the school-rooms in the afternoon, and pupils can then obtain explanations of difficulties.

The Director desires that parents should keep in touch with the teachers of their children, and opportunity for conference is furnished every afternoon. The regular exercises of the morning cannot, of course, be interrupted by callers without detriment.

It is possible for a visitor to get an exalted impression of a teacher by seeing her before a class, even though at the time the pupils may be

Importance of English and History.

sent empty away. A superior class-exercise may make but an indifferent impression upon one who is not in touch with the lessons that have passed and are to come.

It is a part of the plan of the School to reduce home-study as much as possible, to have all the instruction given by the teachers, and to place no unnecessary obstacle in the way of the pupils. Every subject, as has been well said, has inherent difficulties enough for discipline.

The School will not undertake to press the pupils by putting upon them an amount of work greater than that provided by the schedule. Feverish haste will not be encouraged.

Reviews form a means of testing the extent of the pupils' acquaintance with the subjects and their ability to apply their knowledge.

The importance of the studies of English and History as a means of cultivating the taste and of disciplining the mind leads THE CAMBRIDGE SCHOOL to give the greatest attention to them. A special object is to create an appreciation of

Careful Early Training Given.

English writing as an expression of life, and as an illustration of literary form.

Every teacher is an instructor in English, and the written exercises in all departments are criticised with reference to purity of diction as well as to subject matter. Reading is a means of extending acquaintance with Literature. The attempt is made to cultivate the old-fashioned art of reading aloud.

It is the particular aim to make the written expression of thought as natural as the spoken. This is impossible without much practice. Subjects are selected from those about which the pupils have some information, so that they shall not compile formal essays from books. The various courses are conducted with a view to their influence upon each other. Too much stress can hardly be laid upon the importance of careful training in the earlier years.

The arrangements are such that a pupil can continue her studies in unbroken connexion as long as is desired.

Academic and Classical Courses.

The Departments.

There are two principal departments. Elective courses are planned for pupils who need them, by making combinations of studies.

I. THE ACADEMIC DEPARTMENT.

Pupils between twelve and twenty-five years of age.

Reading.	English.	French.
Spelling.	Physics.	German.
Writing.	The Fine Arts.	Latin.
Vocal Training.	Physical Geography.	
Geometry.	Geology.	
Arithmetic.	Physiology.	
Algebra.	Mental Science.	
Trigonometry.	Astronomy.	
History.	Zoölogy.	
Drawing.	Advanced Geography.	

The History of English Literature. Critical Reading of English and American Authors.

☞ Two languages besides English, and one Science, are allowed in the Academic Department. There is an extra charge for more.

Pupils are expected to limit themselves to an average of four class exercises a day for which preparation is needed.

Graduate and Preparatory Courses.

THE CLASSICAL COURSE.

Preparatory for College.

French.	(Three years.)	Greek.	(Three years.)
German.	(Three years.)	Algebra.	(Two years.)
History.	(Two years.)	Geometry.	(Two years.)
Latin.	(Five years.)	English.	(Five years.)
	Physics. (Two years.)		

Pupils who are to be fitted for college, must take at least two years for preparation, unless they have passed the Preliminary Examination, or have done work equivalent to that which it demands.

☞ Pupils who wish to take the college course in three years, may fit themselves for examination in the work of the Freshman year, and thus enter with advanced standing. All College candidates are encouraged to take the Freshman work in English in the School. This has become the established custom in The Cambridge School.

II. THE GRADUATE OR SEMINARY DEPARTMENT.

This is for graduates of schools who wish to continue their studies, but do not wish to go to college. The students are usually from seventeen to twenty-five years of age.

English.	History.	French.
Greek.	Biology.	German.
Latin.	The Fine Arts.	Mathematics.
Mental Science.	Physics.	Physiology.
	Chemistry and Astronomy.	

Lectures on the History of the Fine Arts are given in the Academic Department without charge. They are illustrated with casts, photographs, engravings and drawings.

The Courses Elective.

THE PREPARATORY DEPARTMENT.

A few girls under twelve years of age are trained for the higher classes.

English.	Elementary Science.
Reading.	Arithmetic.
Writing.	Geometry.
Spelling.	Drawing.

French or German.

Exercises in the use of the voice.

Geography,— modelling and the study of maps and globes.

☞ One language besides English, and one Science, are allowed in this Department. There is an extra charge for more.

The younger children have the quiet and care of a small school added to those advantages which can be provided only in a large institution.

It is to be noted that there is no "Course of Study" to which all pupils are confined, but that the subjects are "elective." Individual instruction and freedom of choice are limited by the judgment of the Director, in connexion with that of the parents.

The course is fitted to the pupil — not the pupil to the course.

Conditions for the Admission of Day Pupils.

☞ *Places are engaged for the year. It is a part of the agreement on admission that the pupil shall not be withdrawn before the beginning of the summer vacation, and that there shall be no deductions from the fees.*

Strangers applying for admission must be introduced to the Director, and give the names of their previous schools.

All candidates are expected to show their fitness for the courses for which they apply, before admission to them.

For pupils under twelve years of age the fee is one hundred dollars a year. With two languages besides English, one hundred and twenty-five dollars.

For pupils between the ages of twelve and fifteen years, one hundred and fifty dollars. With more than two languages besides English, one hundred and seventy-five dollars.

For all over fifteen years of age the fee is two hundred dollars each year.

In Laboratory courses there is a fee of five dollars for materials and breakage, payable in advance.

Fees for tuition are to be paid in advance, in two instalments, October first and February first. There are *no deductions* for late entrance, for absences, for premature withdrawal, or for other reasons. Absence and tardiness cause extra work for the School.

☞ All pupils are expected to remain in the school building until the hour of dismissal.

Conditions of Residence.

All the privileges of residence, and tuition in all Branches offered, are provided for $1000 a year.

Places may be engaged at any time.

Bills are payable in advance:

On engaging a place for the year	$ 50.
On the first of October	450.
On the first of February	500.

There are charges for services demanded when dentistry is to be attended to, when meals are served in bed-rooms, and when nurses are needed.

Engagements do not terminate till the long vacation begins. There are no deductions for late entrance, for absences, for premature withdrawal, or for other reasons.

Absences, late entrances, and all other irregularities lay additional burdens on the School.

The young ladies attend such entertainments in Boston and Cambridge as their parents desire, under proper chaperonage.

The modern school year is very brief, and parents are specially urged to arrange to have their daughters arrive in season for the exercises of the first day of each term, and to remain until the close of the term.

In applying for admission, candidates will present the name of the school last attended.

"It would hardly be too much to say that the whole problem of education is how to surround the young with good influences."

The Residences

OF THE CAMBRIDGE SCHOOL.

MARGARET WINTHROP HALL and HOWELLS HOUSE are the Residences of *The Cambridge School*. The first is at No. 21 Chauncy Street, and the second at No. 37 Concord Avenue.

Young ladies who are *properly introduced to the Director* are admitted to these houses.

It is the intention that the Residences shall always be centres of elevating influences. Such a home is to be desired for every young woman, and for those destined to occupy positions of social influence it is indispensable. The ladies in charge of these homes are able to conduct them with a freedom that would be impracticable were the numbers greater; and their influence

Refinement not Learned from Books.

upon the young ladies is more personal, kindly, thorough and effective. Cultivation, good breeding and refinement are not learned from books; the hope for their development lies in association with those whose own lives have been passed with the intelligent and the refined.

Young people cannot be cared for to the best advantage in masses, and the boarding-house and hotel phases of social life are not normal.

The family life is natural for the young woman, and that is offered in the Residences of THE CAMBRIDGE SCHOOL. The young ladies are *in all respects* under the care of the Heads of the homes and of the Director, the purpose being to train them in correct habits and deportment.

The experience of the Director of The Cambridge School, which was for years in Radcliffe College, shows him more and more the exceptional advantages that Cambridge possesses in the way of instruction and cultivation. The beauty of the region is well known. Its historic interest and its intellectual pre-eminence are also familiar.

The Advantages of Eastern Massachusetts.

The beginnings of our National history may be impressively studied, also, in such places as Plymouth, Salem, Lexington and Concord.

Many popular lectures in the halls of Harvard University are open to the public, and afford delightful means of obtaining information upon subjects not so readily and agreeably studied elsewhere. Lectures, concerts and other entertainments in Boston are easily accessible.

Almost every distinguished visitor from foreign lands is seen and heard in the University town. The young ladies in the School have, therefore, unusual opportunities for becoming acquainted with the progress of the world in scholarship,— and seeing men and women of note is no mean part in this general privilege.

"Eastern Massachusetts," it has been said, "is probably the most highly organized community in the world. There is no district of equal size, containing both an urban and a rural population, where the wealth is greater *per capita*. There is no similar district where there is a higher level of

The Advantages of a Home in Cambridge.

popular intelligence, and there is probably none where there is a larger amount of the higher culture without which the best popular education is unattainable. Nowhere in the United States is there the same amount of intellectual and material energy, of will and intelligence, expended in the development of the human individual."

A home in Cambridge enjoys the fresh air and light of the country, with the addition of the advantages of the city, for the frequented portions of Boston are as convenient of access from Cambridge as they are from many of the best residential parts of Boston itself.

Active young women in their plastic age need not only the work of the class-room, but also something adapted to keep the mind in healthful operation outside of school-hours. If the intellectual and social activity of the place in which the school is established do not supply this, it must be sought from other sources. This must be so in an inactive rural town, where the companionship is too often limited to the members of the school household.

Healthful Occupation out of School.

A place like Cambridge, on the contrary, supplies the demand in full measure; the minds of the pupils are occupied in a healthful way at all times, even when they are not in the school-rooms, and the danger of their becoming trivial or morbid is removed, or at least greatly lessened.

The young ladies living in the Residences constitute small family circles, where every member is engaged in a congenial pursuit and is expected to be willing to add to the good cheer.

It is presumed that all who apply for admission will be in sympathy with the general purpose, and it is intended to admit no one, and retain no one, who is not a harmonious member of the household.

The Director attends the Chapel of the Episcopal Theological School. It is an academic chapel, with sittings reserved for the students of Harvard and Radcliffe Colleges, and The Cambridge School, with their Officers and Instructors.

Lectures, Readings, Concerts, etc.

Lectures are given each year under the auspices of Harvard University to which the young ladies attending THE CAMBRIDGE SCHOOL are admitted without charge. They vary from year to year, and are not announced until about the time of their occurrence. More than sixty such opportunities are sometimes afforded during the year.

A series of concerts by the Boston Symphony Orchestra, sustained by the munificence of Henry L. Higginson, Esq., of Boston, is given every winter in Sanders Theatre of Harvard University.

THE RESIDENCES FURNISHED.

The residences are furnished, and young ladies are not required to supply any articles of silver, linen or household goods.

INCIDENTAL EXPENSES.

A deposit must be made by each pupil with the Head of the Residence, to be used in paying such incidental expenses as her parents authorize. This is to be renewed when exhausted. Twenty-five dollars is the usual sum.

"The mind without sympathy and interest is like the sea-anemone when the tide is down, an unlovely thing, closed against external influences, enduring existence as best it can."

R. H. QUICK.

The School Work.

The Academic Department.

The courses of study here announced exhibit actual work; but the school does not hold itself obliged to form classes in every one in the same year.

Pupils are expected to limit themselves to an average of four class exercises a day which require preparation.

I. ENGLISH.

English is studied with the same systematic thoroughness that has been usual in classical work. It is given the first position because it is our instrument for acquiring other learning and wisdom and for communicating them.

The intention is to cultivate, as far as possible, the linguistic and the literary sense; that is, the faculty by which one instinctively appreciates the genius of the language and its literature.

The linguistic sense can be based only on living forms which are met frequently and in a variety of circumstances.

The principles of Composition or Rhetoric are taught in connexion with the study of representative authors.

Frequent themes are required, that the student may secure clearness, directness and simplicity of expression in written language.

In Literature the work is not so much a critical study of form, as an investigation of the spirit of the different productions, which are

Work in English.

considered as exponents of life and character. Much reading is done outside of the class-room, and the recitations are thus left free for the expression of individual thought.

1. Word-formation. Relations between Words. Study of Sentences. Themes, Criticism, Original Work. Readings from English and American Classics.

2. Sentence and Paragraph Structure. Choice of Words. Themes, Criticism, Original Work. Reading required for admission to College; the Harvard examinations begun.

3. History of the English Language. Influence of Latin, Celtic, Scandinavian and Norman French. Themes, Criticism, and Original Work. Reading required for admission to College continued.

4. Native and Foreign Elements in the English Language. Prefixes and suffixes. Themes, Criticism, Original Work. Reading required for admission to College finished.

5. English *A;* the required work of the first year of Harvard College. *Composition:* Hill's Principles of Rhetoric (edition of 1895), practice in writing. *Literature:* Swift's Battle of the Books and Gulliver's Travels; Defoe's Robinson Crusoe (Part I); The Sir Roger de Coverley Papers in The Spectator; Pope's Rape of the Lock, Epistle to Arbuthnot, and Iliad I, VI, XXII; the Lives of Swift, Defoe and Pope in the English Men of Letter Series; Thackeray's English Humorists and Henry Esmond.

Primarily for Graduates. Elective.

6. English Literature from 1400–1558. English Literature from 1558–1637. English Literature from 1637–1700.

7. English Literature from 1700–1745. English Literature from 1740–1797. Wordsworth and Contemporaries 1797–1850.
   These courses to be studied with reference to forms of the Language; as examples of Literature and in their relation to the History and the thought of the period.

Courses in History.

8. English Language and Literature to 1400.

9. The Round Table. Leisurely study of a few authors under the supervision of the Director.

*** The work of each year is supplemented by readings from representative authors in poetry and prose.

There are many Lectures given by Harvard College which are open to the pupils of The Cambridge School without charge.

II. HISTORY.

History is held to include Historical Geography and Map-drawing; and the comparative method, which makes much collateral reading necessary, is followed. Class-work is largely the discussion of the subject-matter. Both lessons and reviews are topical.

The two objects aimed at in teaching History are: 1. To make the subject stimulating to the pupil's imagination and suggestive of thought. 2. To give a basis for future generalizations by supplying accurate and well-arranged facts.

In the study of History the effort is made to train the student to habits of observation and of individual judgment. The use of text-books and the exercise of the memory are not discarded, but such work is supplemented by lectures, discussion and reference to various authorities, especially, when possible, to those contemporary with the period studied. The pupils are encouraged to compare the institutions and statesmen of ancient and modern times, and to consider the life and character of the people in question. A correct use of the mother-tongue in the expression of thought is insisted upon in both oral and written exercises. Separate topics are assigned to the different students and oral reports made by them are subjected to class criticism.

1. Greece. Elementary. Principal Events. Heroes and Leaders. Text-book, Myers's "Eastern Nations and Greece," and Pennell's Greece. Smith's Smaller History of Greece, and Fyffe's Primer.

2. Rome. Elementary. Principal Events. Heroes and Leaders. Manners and Customs. Text-book, Robinson's "A First History of Rome."

Vocal Training.

3. England. Important Events. Political and Legal Institutions. Text-books, Gardiner's Student's History of England, and Guest's Lectures.

4. American History for older pupils, with particular reference to Legal and Political Affairs and Institutions. Causes and Results of the Chief Events. Text-books, Johnston's History of the United States, Fiske's History of the United States, and Thomas's History of the United States.

5. Review of Courses One and Two for the Harvard entrance examinations.

6. Review of Courses Three and Four for the Harvard entrance examinations.

Primarily for Graduates.

7. General History. This course is adapted to the needs of older pupils who may have omitted some of the preceding courses, or who wish to review the subjects in a comprehensive manner. Myers and Allen's General History is used as an outline.

8. French History. Duruy's "History of France," illustrated and amplified by reference to Michelet, Taine, Guizot, Carlyle and others.

9. German History. An advanced course based upon the Epoch Series, Charlton Lewis's "A History of Germany," Baring-Gould's Story of Germany, and other works.

10. American History. Period of the Constitution. Text-books, Johnston's History, Hart's "The Formation of the Union," Fiske's "Critical Period of American History."

III. VOCAL TRAINING.

The main purpose of the course is to cultivate a correct pronunciation, and a rational and forcible method in expression by voice and action. Exercises are given to develop strength, quality, flexibility, and compass in the voice, and correct attitude and carriage of the body. The relation of attitude to vocal expression is studied in connexion with this work. Exercises are given to develop symmetry and grace

Courses in Mathematics.

in general movements of the body. A study is made of the laws governing general expression, and of the special office of gesture. One exercise a week is given in the Preparatory and one in the Academic Department, by Mr. J. J. Hayes, Instructor in Elocution in Harvard College. All pupils are expected to take this course; though candidates for College may omit it during the last two years of the preparatory studies.

The following titles indicate the range of the critical readings given by Mr. Hayes. Much Ado About Nothing, The Lady of the Lake, The Deserted Village, Enoch Arden, The Vision of Sir Launfal, The Courtship of Miles Standish, Irving's Sketch-Book, Evangeline, In a Balcony, Hamlet.

IV. MATHEMATICS.

In teaching Mathematics the aim is to develop the spirit of inquiry, the habit of accuracy in reasoning, and the love of truth; thus giving the subject an important bearing on every other part of the curriculum. Assumptions count for naught with the pupil properly trained in Mathematics. Logical thought is cultivated.

Throughout the course original work is encouraged and set rules are avoided. There are frequent written reviews,— so frequent, and given after such careful preparation, as to make these occasions pleasant opportunities for trial of skill. The pupils are encouraged to rely as little as possible upon text-books.

1. First Year. Arithmetic. Percentage, Interest, Ratio and Proportion, Evolution and Involution.
2. Elementary Geometry. Drawing to scale. Laws of triangles and a few of their simple applications.
3. Second Year. Algebra is begun, and completed.
4. Fourth Year. Plane Geometry. This class is usually preparing for Harvard entrance examinations. Text-book used only in review. Professor Byerly's edition of Chauvenet.
5. Algebra reviewed for College admission examinations.
6. Geometry reviewed for College admission examinations.

Primarily for Graduates.

7. Fifth Year. Logarithms, Trigonometry, and Analytic Geometry. This course prepares for the advanced entrance examination

Courses in German.

at Harvard. Wells's Plane Trigonometry, Sever's Problems in Plane Trigonometry, Briggs's Elements of Analytic Geometry.

V. GERMAN.

The chief object in the course in German is to enable the pupils to read the language at sight and to converse and write with idiomatic ease, founding their knowledge on a thorough acquaintance with grammatical rules.

1. Eysenbach's Grammar. Memorizing German poetry and prose. Reading Kleine Erzählungen (Bernhardt). Immensee (Storm).

2. Eysenbach's Grammar. Conversation and memorizing. Reading Kleine Erzählungen (Bernhardt). Immensee (Storm).

3. Collar's Eysenbach. Conversation. Reading Kleine Erzählungen (Bernhardt). Immensee (Storm).

4. College preparatory class. First year. Eysenbach's Grammar. Memorizing German poetry and prose. Reading Kleine Erzählungen (Bernhardt). Immensee (Storm). Im Zwielicht (Bernhardt).

Primarily for Graduates.

5. College preparatory class. Second and third years. Reading the prescribed books for advanced examination. Translation at sight of modern German prose. Compositions based upon the following books: Riehl (Der Fluch der Schönheit); Freytag (Aus dem Staat Friedrichs des Grossen); Heine (Die Harzreise); Goethe (the first three books of Dichtung und Wahreit); Lessing (Minna von Barnhelm); Schiller (Wilhelm Tell, Das Lied von der Glocke). Thirty pages of lyrics and ballads.

VI. FRENCH.

The instruction in French begins with object lessons. The young pupils are taught the names of familiar things, and are led to use them in simple sentences. The next step is the acquisition of a vocabulary which is put to immediate use in written translations from French

Courses in French.

into English and *vice versa*. A small, easy grammar is then taken up, much attention being given to correctness, based upon a thorough understanding of a few rules. Idiomatic expressions and nice grammatical distinctions come later, and much stress is laid upon careful translations from English into French, in order that the pupil may not only understand French when spoken, but may use it readily herself.

Conversation is insisted upon from the beginning, and exercises in dictation, in letter-writing and in the reading of the choicest productions of modern French authors are constant throughout the course. So far as practicable the class-room exercises are conducted in French. It is intended that the pupils shall have the ability to read French without translation.

1. Younger beginners. Grammar. Whitney's Practical French. Reading: La Lizardière. (Henri de Bornier.)

2. Older beginners. Grammar. Whitney's Practical French. Verbs. (Castaréde.) Dialogues. Familiar Conversations. Reading: Le Chant du Cygne (Ohnet). La Maison de Penarvan (J. Sandeau).

3. Grammar. Chardenal's Complete French Course. Verbs. Pour une Epingle (Saint Germain).

4. Grammar. Chardenal's Second Course. Verbs. Dictation. Anecdotes. Dialogues. Voyage à Paris. Reading: La Perle Noire. La Duchesse Couturière (Comédie). Vaillante (Jacques Vincent). La Lizardière (Henri de Bornier).

5. Grammar. Whitney's Practical French. Verbs. Conversation. Le Maître de Forge (Georges Ohnet).

6. Grammar. Chardenal's Second Course. Verbs. Dialogues. Voyage à Paris. Translations at sight. Reading: Les Enchantements de la Forêt (Theuriet). La Princesse Verte. Les Sabotiers. Jolie Propriété à Vendre (Gréville).

7. Grammar. Kastner's Elements of French Composition. Verbs. Sight Translations. Hennequin's Idioms. Dictation. Reading: Quatre-vingt-treize (V. Hugo). Terre de France (Julliot). Le Bourgeois Gentilhomme (Molière). Les Plaideurs (Racine).

The Importance of Science.

8. Grammar. Chardenal's Second Course. Verbs. Reading: Le Protégé de Marie Antoinette (Marmière). Contes Choisis (Daudet). Mlle. de la Seiglière (Sandeau). Columba (Mérimée).

Primarily for Graduates.

9. Grammar. Roulier's Second Book of French Composition. Sight translation of modern French prose. Dictation. Reading: Horace (Corneille). Andromaque (Racine). Fables, Books I and II (La Fontaine). L'Avare (Molière) Marianne (George Sand). Bataille de Dames (Scribe et Legouvé). Mlle. de la Seiglière (Sandeau). Dosia (Henri Gréville).

10. Blouet's Class-Book of French Composition. Demogeot's Littérature. La Chanson de Roland Chantes Lyriques des Troubadours et des Trouvères. Morceaux Choisis de Théâtre du Moyen Age. Le Cid, Cinna, Horace, Polyeucte (Corneille); Andromaque, Britannicus; Mithridate, Athalie (Racine); Les Précieuses Ridicules, Les Femmes Savantes, Tartufe (Molière); Oraison Funèbre d'Henriette d'Angleterre, Extracts du Discours sur l'Histoire Universelle (Bossuet); Les Fables de La Fontaine, Les Lettres de Mme. de Sévigné. Morceaux Choisis de Descartes; Pascal; Voltaire; Rousseau.

COURSES IN SCIENCE.

A liberal education includes some acquaintance with the constitution of the world in which we live, with the forces that surround us, and with the laws of matter and of life. The laws and principles by which these subjects are explained are beautiful and far-reaching in their application, and the processes of thought required in their study are vigorous and stimulating, and stand in close relation to the intellectual needs of intelligent beings.

VII. CHEMISTRY.

1. An elementary course dealing with the fundamental principles of the non-metals, and a few of the more interesting metals. The

Courses in Science.

chemistry of the atmosphere, of water and of combustion, is made prominent. Laboratory work by pupils. Results kept in note-books. Text-book, Williams's Introduction to Chemical Science.

2. A study of Qualitative Analysis. The general reactions for each group are studied. An unknown substance is given for analysis at the completion of the study of each group. The reactions in all cases are written by the pupils, and corrected by the teacher. Text-books, Stoddard's Outline of Qualitative Analysis, Qualitative Analysis (Fresenius), Manual of Qualitative Analysis (Caldwell and Babcock).

Primarily for Graduates.

3. Advanced work in Qualitative Analysis, and simple Gravimetric and Volumetric Determinatives. Text-books, Qualitative Analysis (Fresenius), Quantitative Analysis (Fresenius).

VIII. PHYSICS.

1. Elementary course, taught chiefly by the inductive method, designed for general students, and preferred for those who are preparing for college. Candidates for college complete their preparation by taking course 2 the second year. About two hundred simple experiments are performed by the students. Gage's Elements of Physics.

2. Second year. Gage's Elements completed and reviewed, with additional problems.

3. A course of not less than forty experiments in Mechanics, Sound, Light, Heat and Electricity required for the Radcliffe admission examinations.

4. This course consists of experimental work alone, for which collateral preparation is required. Text-book, Gage's Physical Laboratory Manual and Note-book.

IX. GEOLOGY.

1. An introductory course, based upon the text-books of R. S. Tarr.

2. Physical Geography. A course leading to the examinations for admission to Bryn Mawr College. Written papers, drawing and

Physiology, Psychology, and Botany.

field work. Russell Hinman's Eclectic Physical Geography.

3. Geography for advanced pupils. Books of travel, field excursions, together with study of Tarr's Geology.

X. ZOÖLOGY.

1. The course consists of laboratory work, based upon type-animals from the protozoa to vertebrates. Microscopic work, dissections and written descriptions. Packer's Zoölogy used for reference.

Primarily for Graduates.

2. Advanced work consisting of recitations, discussions, and thesis writing based upon Darwin's Origin of Species, Descent of Man, and Variation under Domestication, with collateral reading.

XI. PHYSIOLOGY.

1. An elementary course, illustrated by the use of the microscope and by dissections. Dissections and Drawings are made by the pupils, under the direction of the teacher. Martin's The Human Body is the text-book.

Primarily for Graduates.

2. A more advanced course. Comparative Anatomy. Several hours a week are given to laboratory work. Comparative Anatomy and Physiology.

XII. PSYCHOLOGY.

1. A simple introduction to Psychology. The course consists of recitations, discussions and occasional papers upon given topics. Text book, James's Briefer Course in Psychology, with Ladd, Ziehen, and others for reference.

XIII. BOTANY.

1. A simple study of plant life from seeds, seedlings and buds, together with laboratory work and simple analytical work. Microscope and pencil are supplemented by Gray's Lessons.

Astronomy and The Fine Arts.

Primarily for Graduates.

2. Advanced work. A study of the flowering plants, with laboratory and microscopic work and drawings. Text-book, Students Text-book of Botany (Vines).

3. A course in Cryptogamic Botany. Hand-book, Bennett and Murray's Cryptogamic Botany.

XIV. ASTRONOMY.

1. Elements of Descriptive Astronomy without mathematics. Attention is given to Physical Astronomy in its recent advances. Lockyer, Young, Thornton and others, are used as guides.

XV. DRAWING.

Drawing is taught with the intention of helping the pupil to an appreciation and expression of Art. Although Art is too subtle a thing to be analyzed and reduced to rules, yet the mind of the pupil may be so stimulated by certain exercises as to enable her to appreciate beauty and to produce beautiful effects.

It is the intention that each drawing of the pupil shall be a result of feeling and of an appreciation, be it ever so slight, of some principle of beauty.

The first exercises consist of arrangements of straight lines, flowers, fruit and landscape. After line-relations, studies of light and dark are made, in which two tones express as much as possible, and the way is thus led to many tones.

The more difficult study of color in simple tone-values follows. Finally, as the pupil acquires power to express an idea, the desire to draw accurately develops, and the careful work of drawing from casts and still-life may be taken up.

XVI. THE FINE ARTS.

Primarily for Graduates.

1. Travel Class. In this course the Art, History and Geography of the different countries of Europe are studied for the purpose of making intelligent travellers. The course is also profitable for

Value of the Classics.

those who have travelled in Europe, for it is adapted to fix in the mind the impressions that might be forgotten.

At the close of the course, a party of two of three of the students will be taken abroad by one of the teachers of The Cambridge School if desired.

2. European Artists and Galleries. One lecture a week on the technical terms of art; its history and development as seen in the several schools. The course is illustrated with photographs, and serves as a preparation for foreign travel. The pupils are assisted in making collections of photographs of the works studied.

The Classical Course.

Latin and Greek are not regarded as dead languages, except in the sense that all language of books not of our era is dead. They are living in the sense that the English of Chaucer and the Italian of Dante are alive,— dead only to those to whom, for lack of knowledge, they are sealed books.

The aim in teaching should be to have the pupil learn to read the language from the foreign standpoint, to comprehend the idea in its foreign form without the intervention of the English word.

As each nation has left the impress of its character and history upon its language, the life and nature of the people who spoke it are better understood by following this method of reading throughout. Much discussion of the foreign idiom and much comparison are necessary, however, and the comparative study of grammar and expression should accompany all reading. Translation is used at first to ensure accuracy and afterward as a separate exercise in the fluent and graceful use of English.

Mr. Lowell, who was a great teacher, as well as a great poet and critic, has said :—" In reading such books as chiefly deserve to be read in any foreign language, it is wise to translate consciously and in words as we read. There is no such help to a fuller mastery of our vernacular. It compels us to such a choosing and testing, to so nice a discrimination of sound, propriety, position and shade of meaning, that we now first learn the secret of the words we have been using or misusing

The Value of Latin.

all our lives, and are gradually made aware that to set forth even the plainest matter as it should be set forth is not only a very difficult thing, calling for thought and practice, but an affair of conscience as well. Translation teaches us as nothing else can, not only that there is a best way but that it is the only way."

Conscious translation need not, however, accompany all reading in a foreign language. The foreign idiom may become one's own so thoroughly that translation is superfluous.

It is the aim of THE CAMBRIDGE SCHOOL to give its pupils the ability to read Latin and Greek authors in this enjoyable way, and to lay the foundation for agreeable study of them in after life.

XVIII. LATIN.

A knowledge of Latin, though the study is elective, is deemed of importance to most students; for through it they learn the history and meaning of many words in daily use, while they gain the best insight into the fundamental principles of Grammar. It is also an efficient aid in training the mind in habits of exact thought. It is recommended that no student should entirely omit this subject, even in a literary course. Pupils who study Latin take up the subject at the age of twelve, after two years or more of French.

1. For young beginners. Grammar and translation of short sentences. Text-book, Collar and Daniell's First Latin Book.

2. Older beginners, preparing for preliminary examinations in Latin in two years. Collar and Daniell's First Latin Book is used during the first half-year. The reading of Caesar's Gallic War is begun together with a systematic study of Latin Grammar. There is constant exercise in writing Latin sentences based on the text.

3. Second Year. A continuation of the preceding course. The drill book is completed, followed by the reading of easy Latin prose. Later the study of Caesar is begun together with exercises in translating English into Latin illustrating the ordinary constructions. Collar's The New Gradatim, Rolfe's Viri Romae and Kelsey's Caesar.

Courses in Latin.

4. Two books of Caesar's Gallic War are read during the year, with rigid attention to the grammatical construction. Kelsey's Caesar.

5. The first three books of Virgil's Aeneid are read. The various classical references are discussed and some sight reading is done. Murray, Bulfinch, Smith, Rich, and Guhl and Kohner are used as reference books. Allen and Greenough's Virgil is the text-book.

6. Preparatory class for the Harvard and Radcliffe preliminary examinations. The entire grammar is reviewed; three more books of Cæsar's "Gallic War," selections from Nepos's Lives and Sallust's "Catiline" are read rapidly with frequent exercise in sight-reading. Harvard papers are given for written sightwork. Text-books are Kelsey's Cæsar, Rolfe's Nepos, and Allen and Greenough's Sallust.

7. Virgil and Cicero in preparation for "final examinations" in Latin. Much sight-reading is done in addition to prepared translations. Harvard papers are given as tests. Text-books are Allen and Greenough's Virgil and Cicero.

8. Latin Composition. In preparation for the Radcliffe examinations. Text-book, Collar's Latin Composition, supplemented by similar English passages for translation into Latin.

Primarily for Graduates.

9. Work in Cicero, Livy and Terence, corresponding to the work of the Freshman year in Harvard College. The course corresponds with the Freshman work in Latin in Harvard College. Pupils who do not expect to enter college may take this course, if qualified.

XVIII. GREEK.

1. The previous work in Latin prepares the way for intelligent and rapid work in Greek syntax. The Latin constructions as well

Courses in Greek.

as the English are constantly compared with the Greek. White's Beginner's Greek Book is used. Xenophon's Anabasis is begun in the course of the year.

2. A year's work in reading Xenophon. Work in syntax is kept up. A constant effort is made not to have the text regarded as a detached piece of language, useful only in illustrating curious constructions, but rather to have a knowledge of contemporary Greek history throw light on all allusions, and to reach an appreciation of the intrinsic interest and historical value of Xenophon's simple narrative.

3. The first three books of the Iliad and Books XIII, XVII, XXI of the Odyssey are read. Attention is paid to the variations in form from the Attic dialect and to the derivation of words. Effort is made to arrive at an appreciation of the Homeric spirit, and to translate with ease and accuracy. Harvard papers are given as tests. Seymour's Iliad. Merry's Odyssey.

4. Greek Composition. Translation from English into Greek, dictation and oral exercises based on Xenophon's Hellenica. The course prepares for advanced elective 3 (a) of the Harvard examinations. The text-books are Collar and Daniell's Greek Composition, and Goodwin's Greek Grammar.

Primarily for Graduates.

5. Work in Lysias, Plato, Euripides, and Homer corresponding to the first year's work in Greek in Harvard College. A student by taking this course would be prepared not only for the advanced examinations, but also to enter the sophomore Greek course of Radcliffe College. Students who do not intend to enter college may take this course, if qualified for it.

"To be taught to see is to gain word and thought at once, and both true."
                                                RUSKIN.

Plato saith: *"In every work the beginning is the most important part, especially in dealing with anything young and tender."*

The Preparatory Department.

It is the aim in this department to train the pupils to delight in right habits of study, to cultivate and strengthen their natural powers of observation, and to teach them how to concentrate their attention agreeably upon any work before them.

All available methods are employed to encourage mental alertness and self-activity. The pupils are shown how to investigate for themselves, and the dictionary and other reference-books are familiarly consulted. By such work the pupils are prepared for the higher classes, and it is impressed upon them that thoroughness is necessary to success.

I. ENGLISH.

SPELLING.

The exercises in spelling are both written and oral, and the work is done in connexion with the Reading.

GRAMMAR.

The exercises are based upon Longman's Junior Grammar.

1. Letter-writing. Story-writing. Abbreviations and contractions. Correct use of words.

2. Story-writing. Letter-writing. Parts and kinds of sentences. Beginning parts of speech. Memorizing poetry.

3. Parts of speech. Punctuation. Study of words and their derivations. Composition. Memorizing poetry.

Preparatory Courses.

READING.

1. Seaside and Wayside, III (Wright), Water Babies (Kingsley).
2. Greek Heroes (Kingsley), The Little Duke (Yonge).
3. The Peasant and the Prince (Martineau), Adventures of Ulysses (Lamb), A Midsummer Night's Dream (Shakespeare).

The work in Spelling is done in connexion with Reading. The words studied are taken from the daily reading lessons.

The "Heart of Oak" series of literary Readers, edited by Professor Norton, of Harvard University, is used in this department.

II. GERMAN.

1. German conversation and writing. Memorizing poetry. Reading. The Children's Own German Book.

III. FRENCH.

1. Oral instruction. Words, sentences, reading, games. Pupils are encouraged to ask questions and to make themselves understood without using English to aid them. Text-books, Nouvelle Méthode de Lecture pour Les Enfants.
2. Second Year. Reading, writing, dictation. Bué's First French Book. Le Caniche Blanc. Les Malheurs de Sophie. (La Comtesse de Ségur.)
3. Third Year. Keetel's Elementary Grammar. Contes de Fées. (De Beaumont.) Les Malheurs de Sophie. (La Comtesse de Ségur.)

IV. MATHEMATICS.

It is intended that the work in Arithmetic shall lay the foundation for deductive reasoning, and that the pupils shall be trained by it in the art of thinking. They are to be taught to take nothing for granted, and to understand each step by which their results are obtained. It is not forgotten that the girls are not to be trained to become mathematicians, but rather to comprehend simple arithmetical processes.

Preparatory Courses.

ARITHMETIC.

Oral instruction is followed by supplementary work based upon the text-books. There are written reviews each month.

1. Advanced work in the four rules. Roman numerals.

2. Review of integers. Fractions and Decimals.

3. Wentworth's Grammar School Arithmetic. Review of Fractions and Decimals. Percentage begun.

V. GEOGRAPHY.

A distinguished professor has said that the power to read maps should be the aim in teaching Geography. The molding-board and the relief-map are great helps. The proper use of the English language, oral and written, is constantly cultivated in this study. It trains the imagination at the same time.

It is recognized that "Geography has its highest usefulness in revealing the processes by which the differences of climate, soil, productions, and races of men on the earth arise and develop, and, by a counter process of human industry, are united again through the commerce of the world"; that "its highest lesson is that of the triumph of human mind over the obstacles of nature and even over the limitations of climate and soil." Geography properly taught trains the observing faculty, stimulates the reasoning powers, exercises the memory, teaches the value of classification, excites an interest in familiar objects, gives just conceptions of one's own country and intelligent views of the whole world. To this end such books of reference are used as "A Bird's-Eye View of the World," by Onesime Reclus, "Commercial Geography," by E. G. Chisholm, and Trotter's Lessons in the New Geography, in addition to the usual School Geographies of Longman, Frye, Harper, Appleton and Swinton.

1. Beginners. Frye's Elementary Geography is used as the basis for the work.

Preparatory Courses.

2. The subject is taught chiefly by means of maps and imaginary journeys, together with information gathered by the pupils from many sources. Harper's Geography is the hand-book.

3. A continuation of the preceding course, with the same methods and an additional text-book, The Story of our Continent. (Shaler).

SCIENCE.

Familiar talks are given to the pupils. The intention is to awaken an interest in phenomena by presenting some of the facts of Science in a popular form.

VI. ZOÖLOGY.

A very simple course. The study of the forms and habits of some familiar types of animals, including the hydroids, star-fish, cray-fish, clam, and grass-hopper. Drawings are made from each subject as it is studied.

VII. NATURAL HISTORY.

Laboratory work and talks on Natural History, supplemented by visits to the Agassiz Museum of Harvard University as groundwork. No outside preparation is required.

VIII. PHYSIOLOGY.

Very elementary work. Martin's Human Body (elementary course) is used for reading in class. The text is explained by means of a skeleton, charts, and individual organs of different animals. No outside work is required.

IX. BOTANY.

A study of the principal features of plants and flowers. The main object of the course is to encourage and cultivate observation. Drawing enters largely into the work.

Preparatory Courses.

X. SPECIAL WORK.

WRITING.—Special instruction and practice several times a week. Vertical penmanship is taught.

DRAWING—from objects, as in the Academic Department.

ELOCUTION.—Use of the voice and critical reading, as in the Academic Department, under Mr. J. J. Hayes, of Harvard College.

MYTHOLOGY.—Simple instruction in this subject, as a preparation for Grecian History.

HISTORY.—1. Simple instruction in United States History, as a preparation for the Academic work. Eggleston's Elementary History.
    2. Mythology and ancient monarchies. No single text-book. The subject-matter is taken from various sources furnished by the teacher and the pupils. Bulfinch's Age of Fable carefully studied.

Situation of the Cambridge School.

THE CAMBRIDGE SCHOOL is situated at No. 36 Concord Avenue, near Craigie Street.

The Huron Avenue line of electric railway, from Newton, Watertown and Mount Auburn, runs through Concord Avenue and Garden Street to Tremont Street, Boston, to Bowdoin Square, and to the Providence Station, Park Square, making the distance in about thirty minutes. At Harvard Square, exchange checks are given passengers without charge. *The cars stop at the School, on notice.*

The most agreeable route from Boston to Cambridge is that over the Harvard Bridge connecting with the Huron Avenue line at Harvard Square, Cambridge.

Not far from THE CAMBRIDGE SCHOOL, on Brattle Street, stands the home of Longfellow, the headquarters of Washington when he was in Cambridge at the opening of the Revolutionary war. On the side of the Common formerly stood the house in which the poet Holmes was born, which had served as headquarters for the Committee of Safety at the beginning of the Revolution.

The Huron Avenue cars from Boston for Mount Auburn, Watertown and Newton pass the School and Howells House, as well as Chauncy Street; and those on Massachusetts Avenue pass Chauncy Street also.

Margaret Winthrop Hall is at No. 21 Chauncy Street, about equidistant from Garden Street and Massachusetts Avenue.

Howells House is No. 37 Concord Avenue.

Mr. Gilman's residence is at No. 5 Waterhouse Street.

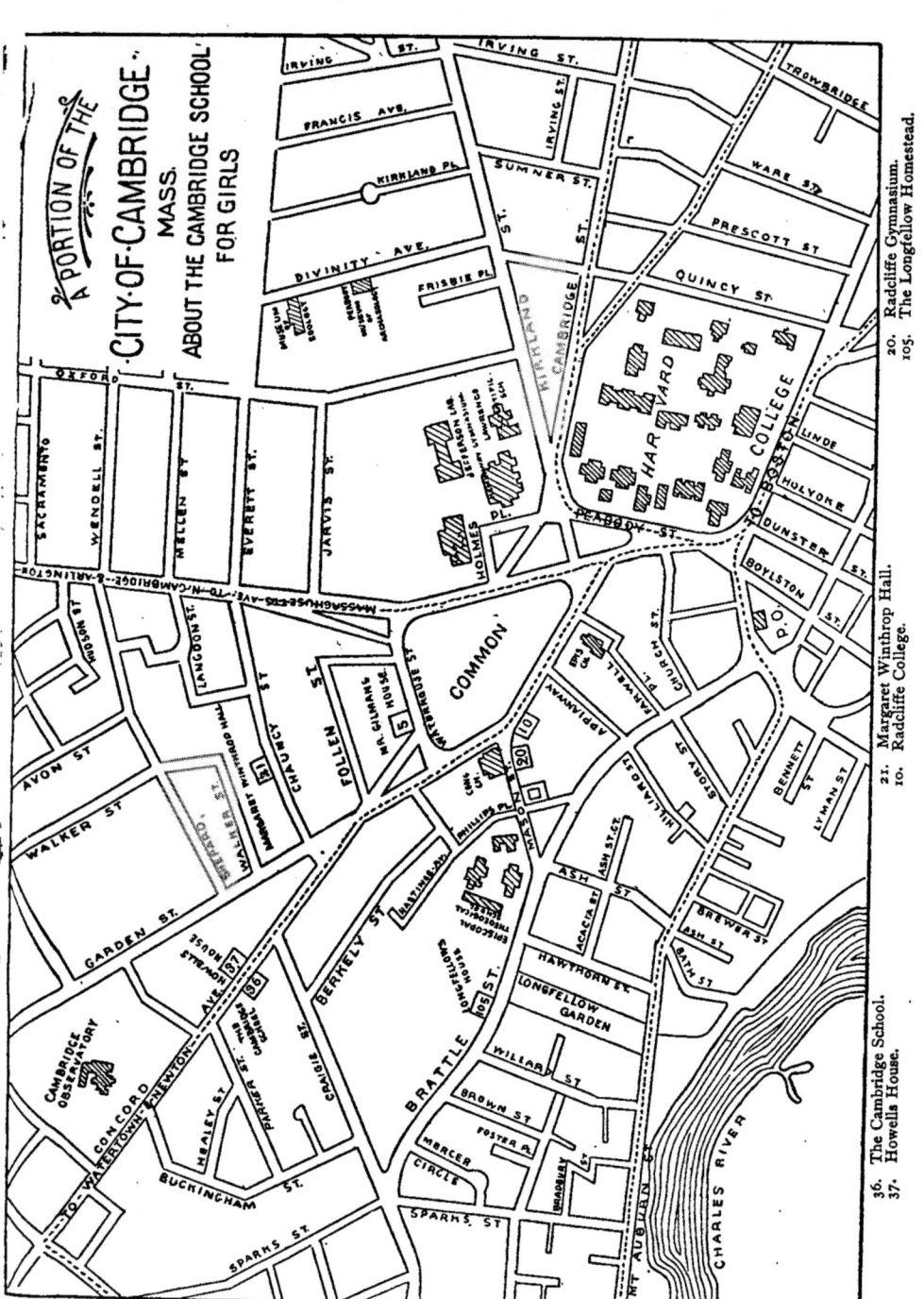

Printed by Libri Plureos GmbH in Hamburg, Germany